Pass the P

Written by Dorothy Avery
Illustrated by Jan van der Voo

The music stops.
Who has the present?

3

The dog has the present.
The dog takes off the blue paper.

4

the pig

the cat

the goat

the horse

the dog

the duck

The music stops.
Who has the present?

7

The goat has the present.
The goat takes off the red paper.

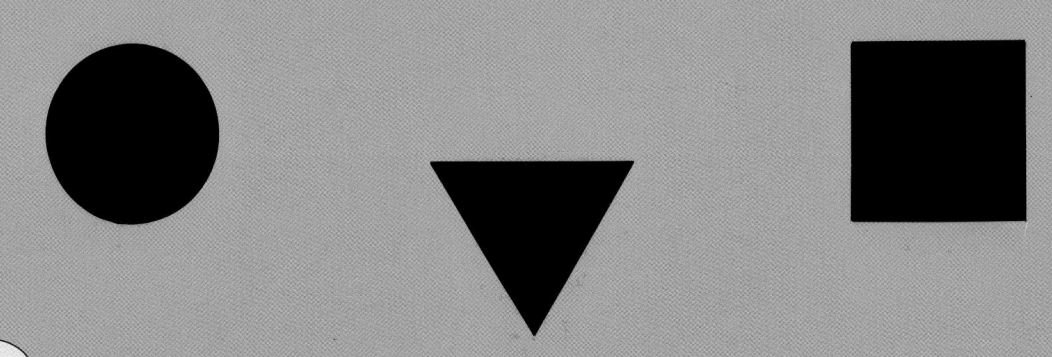

9

The music stops.
Who has the present?

11

The duck has the present.
The duck takes off the yellow paper.

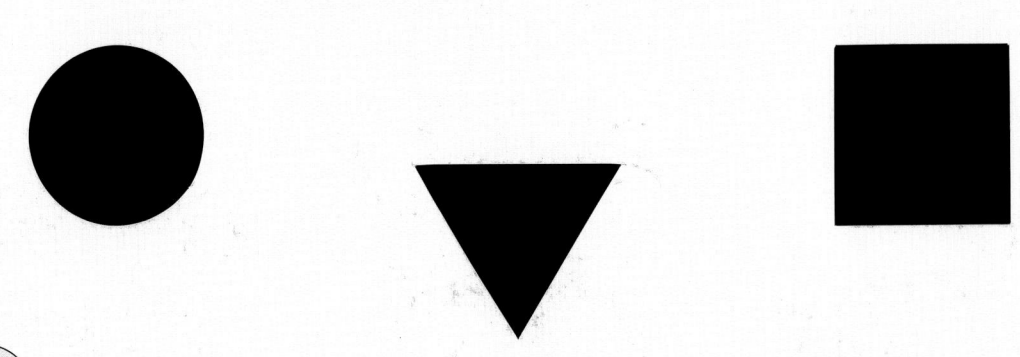

13

The music stops.
Who has the present?

15

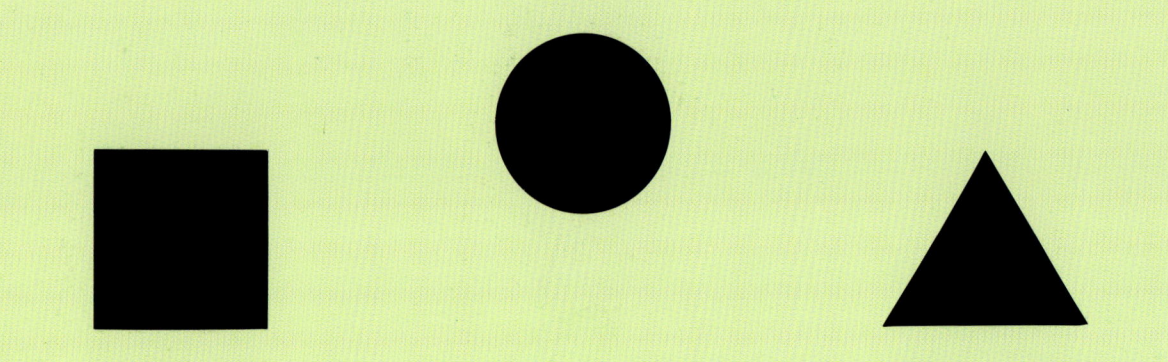

The pig has the present.
The pig takes off the green paper.

17

The music stops.
Who has the present?

19

The cat has the present.

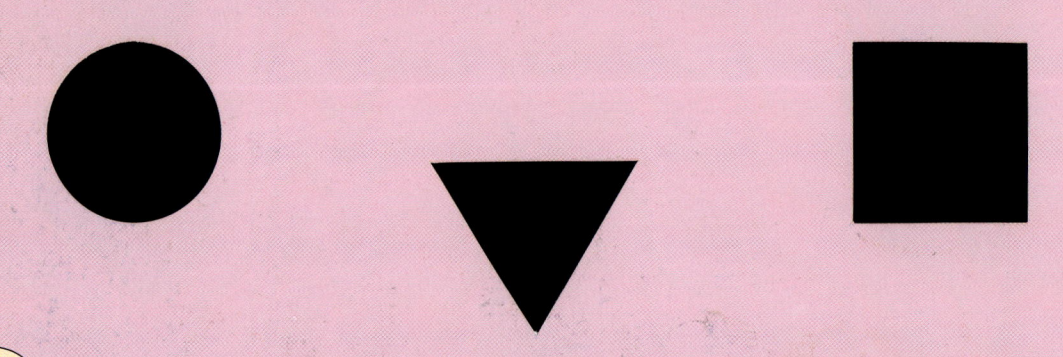

21

The cat takes off
the purple paper.

23

Surprise!